The author was born in Perth but moved to Richmond, Surrey, in 1948 and attended Tiffin School, Kingston. He served in the RAF, followed by 9 years in the Bank of England, then retraining as a Probation Officer. He worked as such in Brixton and Battersea as well as two years in Holloway Prison. Came on promotion to Reading in 1979. He retired early, in 1996 and then spent ten years as a Family Mediator. Since then he has written two novels and several books of worship material, mainly new hymns. Also took a master's degree in Criminal Justice at University of Reading in 1987. He is married to his wife, Janet, for nearly sixty years and has four children. He is still active in local life and church – a lay preacher for sixty years.

With my great respect for all those involved in the Criminal
Justice System, especially the Probation Service.

Colin Ferguson

BEHIND THE CRIME

AUSTIN MACAULEY PUBLISHERS™

LONDON · CAMBRIDGE · NEW YORK · SHARJAH

A CIP catalogue record for this title is available from the British Library.

ISBN 9781528938723 (Paperback)
ISBN 9781528969659 (ePub e-book)

www.austinmacauley.com

First Published (2019)
Austin Macauley Publishers Ltd
25 Canada Square
Canary Wharf
London
E14 5LQ

Part One

Taking the Plunge

It doesn't seem like fifty years ago but it was 1967 when I decided to become a probation officer. A career in the Bank of England seems a long way from working as a probation officer in Brixton, or in Holloway Prison, but this was the journey I took. I could truthfully say that my own unsettled childhood experience often made me feel there but for the grace of God it could have been me on the receiving end.

But here I was at twenty-seven, married with two children and a mortgage when I was struck down with TB and for some time thought, I may never recover. The result was nine months off work and two years of taking things more gently that made me review my life. My voluntary involvement with an open youth club run by a church in Battersea led me slowly to see this as what I was meant to do. Trips to the Juvenile Court with club members led me into contact with the service and I had a high regard for two of my friends who were both in the service.

Three years later, when I was fully fit again, I took a leap of faith from the security and comfort of the bank into the chaotic world of criminal justice.

I couldn't have done it without the wonderful support of my wife, especially as we had two young children at the time. I am sure my mother thought I had gone mad.

Janet shared with me the good days and the more frequent hard days for it was not like the bank, a job where you came home in the evening and that was that. Probation became a way of life and I am so glad that I had the great experience of working with so many dedicated colleagues in both the service and the courts, and of course the people themselves.

Why did I do it? The probation service grew out of the police court missionary services and for me, even though the church connection had long since been replaced by professional training, faith and a strong belief in the worth of everyone were at the core of my decision, and they still are. Even though I, like everyone else, could hate some of the things that they did, I could still retain a respect for them as individuals and believe in the power of hope even in the darkest corners of society.

I suppose that it was meeting with Harry that started me thinking that this was the direction I should follow. He was in hospital with me in 1965 and so it seems right to begin with his story.

Harry and the Angels

He came in with a prison officer attached to his wrist via handcuffs. Thankfully, they were removed before he went for his operation which was for a serious breathing condition.

I was at that time very involved in the local Churches together group and three of my ministerial friends all called to see me at the same time. They were gathered around the bottom of my bed, which was also across from the end of Harry's bed just as he came out of his anaesthetic. They were the first thing he saw and he told me later how he had thought he was dead and now facing the angels who would judge whether he went up or down.

Harry had a long criminal record having started early by being taken by his father on burglaries. His father died in prison before the war and Harry was called up and served in France and North Africa before he was invalided out with a gammy leg and a chest wound which was what still brought him into hospital. His mother sadly, was killed in the blitz.

After the war, he was on his own, unable to walk properly and with no family support he soon began to drift back into crime, especially burglary. He told me, and I had no reason to disbelieve him, that he only burgled for food and any loose money.

Being caught gave him security and prison was therefore not a problem. We felt sorry for Harry who we could see as a casualty of the war and of poor education and homelessness.

Two years later, he was released and we offered him a room to give him a chance to find some security for himself. We knew it was a gamble but we wanted to give him a chance. He was obviously very grateful and went to all his appointments and looked at various options. Sadly, he was unable to get a job as his injury and his record militated against him.

All was fine for nearly a month and then he disappeared with half of our housekeeping money. I always thought that it was a good sign as he could so easily have taken the lot. He also left behind most of his possessions. Poor though they were, the money he had stolen would not have been enough to replace them.

It was three years later when I was rung by the local hospital almoner to say that he was there and that he was dying. He had asked her to ring and to say that he was sorry to have let us down. He died before I was able to get in to see him.

There was no indication of him having been in court for the last three years.

The cynic might say he hadn't been caught but that would have been unusual as the prison was the nearest thing he had to a home. Perhaps our kindness had given him more respect for others and for himself. We were the last people he remembered before he died and that meant something.

It was September 1967, when I started my first practice placement in Tottenham. That experience is told in the following recollection.

Trio

I had made the leap and here I was in North London on my first practice placement. My supervisor was very good and showed me round the courts and made me read all his records to see in particular how to write reports for the court. After only two weeks, he said, "Now it's your turn."

He came with me on my first home visit and I think even he got more than expected. It was simple enough on the surface. A fourteen-year old boy had been charged with stealing a bicycle. He came to see us and it soon became clear he was poorly educated and just wanted to be one of the gang. The home visit was what made it different. His mother was Spanish and had very poor English and his father was deaf and dumb but only spoke sign language in Spanish. It was not a good idea to get the boy to translate for us so his twelve-year-old sister did so. She spoke to mother, she signed to father and back again. It was my first report, checked of course by Kevin, my supervising officer.

I was then given a report to do by myself. "It's a fairly simple one," said Kevin and then he went on holiday for two weeks with me covering for his work. "There shouldn't be much to do and you can always ask Fred for help."

The two brothers, aged fourteen and twelve, were from a travelling family and had been selling wicker baskets on the street. They were just doing what their family always did. Then mother said something about social services.

After a lot of digging, I discovered that the social service records were having trouble following the family.

Two days before my report was due in, I discovered they were well known to a social worker in Suffolk. There was a care order on the older boy going back to when he was seven, when he had been responsible for drowning another child. They were both conditionally discharged for the present offences on condition that Social Services became involved.

Tom was one of Kevin's probationers with a very large family and a horse which pulled his totter's cart as well as a small menagerie in the garden. They lived in an old Victorian mansion. Tom was banned from driving for many years and had therefore taken to a horse and cart to do his totting (rag and bone man).

Tom had called in to see Kevin, but got me instead. He was livid about his oldest daughter being pregnant again. I did very little other than to let him tell me his concern, which bearing in mind, she already had two children did seem over the top. I promised to let Kevin know the moment he returned. Tom was waiting for him on Monday morning.

Fortunately, I had left a note on the top of Kevin's desk. Later I discovered why Tom was so irate. He was the father of his oldest daughter's two children, but not of this one. Those were the easy ones! – Welcome to probation!

West London
The Hostel and Balham

After three months in Tottenham, there was a more intense theoretical training on the Home Office Training course in West London. Success here led me to a more active placement in Balham when I had my own first responsibility for a case from court report on. Finally, I was ready to be released on to the criminal justice world.

First though, was a placement for four weeks in a probation hostel in Kent. Set in the deepest countryside, the Hostel was in fact an old farmhouse and the work was still farming. I was to be as one of the residents for this placement, which meant cleaning the cowshed, feeding the pigs, washing up after the twenty residents had been fed. As an added attraction, we had one of the worst snowfalls for a long time and had to dig ourselves out of the four hundred yards to the gate. Needless to say, the residents thoroughly enjoyed the snow but not the digging.

Not surprisingly, I caught flu and was confined to the house. Just my luck, this was after all the hard work. As I wasn't too badly affected, I soon found a useful task in sorting out the house accounts and by the time I had done that, I was able to return home for Christmas and prepare for my next placement in Balham.

One of my colleagues was about to retire after thirty years because he had suddenly realised that he was supervising the grandson of one of his early cases. He had been in Balham all of his career.

Talking with him made me realise that probation would never be a 9:00 to 5:00 job. As I have often said, I always knew when I had to begin but I never could be sure of when it would end.

Balham was still a fairly protected time as I was again only there for three months and most of the work was in court taking notes and occasionally seeing a referral from the court. Often this would be what was termed a matrimonial case. One never knew what might turn up as one of my female colleagues found out, when one man insisted on showing her where his wife had bitten him. It was such a referral that brought me into contact with Leroy and his wife.

Fussing and Feuding

One of the first such cases showed me where my education proved rather lacking as Leroy Johnson was sent to me. He was a slight man with a very pronounced Jamaican accent which was rich with words that I had to learn quickly. Leroy was the first of many contacts with the black community.

He was in court because his wife had asked for a divorce. They had lived together for some years and only married last year. It was as Leroy put it, "She only got married so she could divorce me. Ever since then, she has been fussing and feuding me." (Which I gathered was giving him hell.) I promised I would write to her and invite her to come and see me as well, which she did.

She was a small quiet woman, who did not seem quite the person who was always 'fussing and feuding' with Leroy. She was concerned that they had no children and it was down to him being too tired when he got home. I offered to talk with them both together and she seemed happy to do so. I was quite unprepared for what was to follow.

Two weeks later, Leroy was back unexpectedly. He had gone to work that morning and come home to an empty house. Not just his wife but everything that could be moved had gone.

A neighbour told him that a furniture lorry had turned up half an hour after he had left and his wife had gone with it.

Their joint account at the bank was also empty and there was no information at all as to where she may have gone. The van had been hired by another black man and she had gone with the van.

Leroy was distraught. He felt dishonoured and betrayed. He paced up and down the office then suddenly left after I had given him some solicitor's names to help him with the legal ramifications. I wrote to him later but there was no reply.

I never saw him again but two years later I had a call from a probation officer in Birmingham. Leroy had remembered my name. Sadly, it was the worst possible news as Leroy had waited for his wife in the morning as she was going to work and stabbed her to death.

Welcome to South Lambeth

My first office as a qualified officer was at Tierney Road, Streatham which sounds all right but was in fact the base for working the whole of South Lambeth from Acre Lane in Brixton, Tooting, Tulse Hill, Streatham and Gypsy Hill. The area was well known for many wrong reasons as the influence of the Krays and the Richardson gangs still hung over the criminal fraternity. It was also the epicentre of the mainly Jamaican immigration. Not the first wave but the coming of the children who had been left at home with grandparents and who now came before they had to pay full fare.

They came to a society that was not prepared for them, and which failed to understand them and as such they soon became alienated, rejected and angry.

Their parents didn't know what to do with them, the schools didn't know how to work with them and they didn't know what was happening, except that they did not like it. Neither the police nor the courts were adequate at dealing with them and responded harshly, which soon helped to create even more disillusion.

For me, it was a steep learning curve though my own slight experience of coming from a Scottish village to live in a single room with my mother and sister, and then having to cope with an abusive and prejudiced school situation which seemed intent on demoralising me, gave me a slight understanding of the devastation of the life they were facing.

The area was then also one of much poverty and crowded housing. Even where we were in more up-market Streatham, one of the most notorious brothels in London was just at the other end of the road.

I was given my own 'case-load' of forty-two probationers which, apart from those on a straight forward probation order, also included youngsters on borstal and detention centre licence. I also had about three reports to write each week for the court and to be in court once a week to pick up cases for referral as well as those who had come for advice. We had also just taken over the prison welfare service, which meant that anyone released from prison could voluntarily ask for our help.

There were six officers there plus a senior manager and a small team of secretarial staff that I soon discovered were the real front line. I was given Edna as my secretary. I wasn't actually scared of her but she was somewhat intimidating and determined to lick me into shape which was probably a good thing.

It took me nearly three months to even find all my 'clients'. Finally, I took the last three cases back to court for what was called a breach of their probation order. I was cycling around the area at the time and failed to get to the South Western Magistrate's before the court session began. That week all three of the missing group turned up.

I continue the stories with a number of oddities.

Oddities

Not everything is worth a chapter because they were as the title says, oddities, Brian for example, was on Borstal license. He had been in a lot of trouble in the past for burglary. On this occasion that he had an appointment with me, it was apparent that he was disturbed. I asked him what was wrong.

"You know that first time I got nicked five year back, well I was with one of my mates but he legged it over the back fence and they never had him, but I just met him again and he's only a ***** copper now."

Billy and one of his friends had stolen a mini-van and driven it around Tooting and Balham all afternoon and were only stopped when they tried to persuade two girls to get into the back of the van. What's so odd about that? Well they were both 11 years old and one worked the steering wheel while the other did the pedals because they weren't tall enough to do both. The case was referred to social services.

When you ask people why they did what they did you do not expect them to say it was because they had a red nose and wanted to get the money for an operation. Clive's problem was one of anxiety and shyness. His nose was perfectly normal. When he was able to drive he got a car and then a girlfriend and never worried about his nose again.

Lofty was just that, 7ft tall. He had several prison sentences and the story was that his trousers had to be passed from one prison to another as they had cut one pair in half to lengthen the legs of another pair. He was an interesting character in that he was a free-lance artist who spent most of his summers in Cornwall, living in a tent and selling his work to tourists. The police would arrest him from time to time for vagrancy and he would be fined. In time, as he never paid the fines he was arrested and sent to prison, which he always seemed to do when the bad weather came.

The Brixton area was not a good place to be at night and when the fifteen year-old sister of one of my clients was gang raped, there seemed so little that anyone could do except to hope that the gang was caught. My 'client' had his own ideas about finding them. Often, that was the way that 'justice' happened.

Courts are not supposed to be funny but occasionally the pontification of some magistrates can be unexpectedly so. The case of 80-year-old Fred who walked round his house naked came about after the council cut down the hedging outside his front room.

The result was that children on their way to school were blessed with a vision of Fred every time he drew his curtains. The court was reasonably sympathetic and gave him a warning and finished by saying, "I am going to give you a conditional discharge but you must promise not to do this again. Now go home and pull your socks up!"

Kevin was a gambler and in heavy debt. He was married, though this was greatly strained and had two children. He had resorted to stealing the family shopping as he had spent the money on another second-place horse. Things came to a head while I was writing the report for the court as he went home one afternoon and thought he would do the hoovering to at least show willing. He couldn't find the hoover and called out to his wife, "Where is the hoover?"

When she appeared at the door, he sensed that all was not right. "They came and took it away."

"How will we clean the carpet?"

"We won't," she replied, "They took that as well." Upon which she slammed the door. A week later, she had started divorce proceedings. As his bed had also been taken away he was then sleeping on the bare floorboards while his wife returned to her mother with the children.

His three-month prison sentence was almost a relief to him but by then she had returned to the flat and changed the locks. I lost contact with him after that as he had to move out of the area to stay with his brother.

Gambling is one of the most insidious addictions of all as you don't look ill but it can have the most terrible effects on family life as well as on the individual. It is one of the main causes of homelessness and can lead to other life destructive addictions and sadly to a high rate of suicide.

Tony was a 'jiggler'. This was a new word for me but he was a professional car thief and had keys filled down to make it easier to open car doors. This time he had been caught with the keys in his possession. His story was very plausible but it soon fell to pieces and was a good lesson for me to be less trusting of the sad story.

He used a form of faction; that is fiction with just enough fact in it to make it believable. The magistrate was not confused. He went to prison for six months.

Writing reports had its hidden pitfalls such as the time I wrote a report on Simon X who was still at school but had become involved in a fight at a local pub. My interviews with him and his family showed that he was following in his father's footsteps. Father was a large bully of a man and had convictions for violence himself, whereas his mother spoilt him. My report described Simon as being dominated by his father and that his mother over indulged him. Father came in to see me after the court hearing and he was very irate. When I pointed out to him that his behaviour to me was exactly what I meant, he stopped, "Nah," he said, "I know that, but his mother doesn't drink that much."

I never used the word 'overindulge' again.

The Sex Crime

Steven was in his early twenties. He had shared an incestuous relationship with his mother from the age of fourteen and this had left him unable to distinguish between fact and fantasy as when he drove his car around without wearing any trousers or underwear and invited young women to join him.

He later committed a rape in a nurse's home but could not recognise the wrongness, insisting that she had 'wanted it'. Even a spell in Grendon Underwood prison with its special psychiatric unit failed to prevent him from reoffending within a month of his discharge.

On probation, he attended as required and talked about his problems but it had no effect on his actual behaviour. He saw me as someone who understood what he was doing, likewise the psychiatrist.

He listened to our words but could not relate them to his behaviour. He returned to prison for a lengthy sentence.

Steven was the first sex offender I had to supervise. Not surprisingly they were among the least successful cases I had to work with because few of them had any sense of wrongdoing. The sex crime is directly aimed at a victim whether it be as Jim who exposed himself along the towpath (wilfully, lewdly and obscenely as the charge puts it) and then ran away or whether it is aimed at molestation of children.

The computer age has given the child pornographer and abuser more opportunity now than anything in the 1960s or '70s. The worst of that age were the men (mostly but not only) who got work in places where children were in some form of care. Many are now paying the price for their historical abuse.

John G was on parole after serving a sentence for a violent sex attack. He reported to see me on his way back from work and then went home to be in by the curfew that had been imposed as a condition of his parole. Looking back, I can now recognise the signs of his danger. He was very correct, a placid personality, did everything he was told. A week after his parole ended, he attacked a young woman in a car park and raped her. The fact he was sentenced to a long prison sentence was no consolation to her, us or his family.

I learned very quickly that you could not take risks with sex offenders and the rules nowadays are entirely appropriate. There is a world of difference between teenage fumbling and grooming young victims. Some as Steven had a deep-rooted psychiatric problem but the man who tries to control his relationships by violence is little better.

Danny and the Dole

Danny had been supervised by almost everyone in the office. He was totally on his own, illiterate, innumerate, unhygienic. Nobody wanted to supervise him, but I was the newcomer and I didn't know him. Danny became my lost cause. He was a very sad cause. Abandoned by his mother when a baby, he was raised in an orphanage in Ireland run by the Christian Brothers. I will not describe their raising of their wards except to say it was neither Christian nor brotherly. When I worked later in Holloway, many of the young women there had come through the same system. Its effect was to destroy their self-confidence and leave them vulnerable to exploitation.

We were his family. He was scared of everyone else and terrified of the social security staff who kept asking him questions that he could not answer, then gave him forms to fill in which he took because they told him to. Being unable to read or write, he simply kept them in a box in the room a social worker had found for him. He had received a letter from them which a friend had read for him. It was demanding the filled in paperwork otherwise his benefit would be stopped. I went with him to the office, which was a first time for me. I sat with him for forty minutes until his name was called.

"Who are you?" asked the officer.

I told him and it was as if a veil had been lifted, "You should have said you were here and we would have seen you sooner."

Suddenly, Danny became somebody. I explained that he was unable to read and that he had a probation order which had been made because of a fraud. It was because he could not understand what he had to do and had been too scared of the policeman to disagree with what he was told. I left them my name and number so that they would have a point of contact for Danny in the future.

Life began to be easier for Danny and demanding on me but I was determined not to give up on him, I found a local Catholic Church where they had teaching sessions for the illiterate and where their opinion of the Christian Brothers was even stronger than mine. Danny enjoyed being in the fellowship of the Church, it was after all, slightly familiar to him.

The next great triumph was to find a job and thankfully this was undemanding and repetitive which is what he could do. Even his landlady became an ally and did his laundry for him. He had to pay for it but it was a step in improving his acceptability.

By enlarging his trustworthy community, Danny began to grow. He did begin to learn basic reading and writing. He found friends in the Church and satisfaction in his job. Even the Social Security discovered that a bit of time explaining what was needed, paid off because once he had it in his head it became part of his pattern.

His probation order came to an end and a year later when I left the area he had not come back.

Polly – Sometimes Justice Is Not Enough

Polly was only twenty when I met her. She was on probation with a condition that she stayed in a probation hostel in our area. Her home was in Liverpool and so were her two very young children. She had been in care from the age of fourteen having been placed there following her mother's death from an overdose of drugs. At seventeen and already the mother of her first child, she was found a small flat on the tenth floor of a high-rise block.

It wasn't long before she was pregnant again. She loved her children but had very little idea of how to care for them and her boyfriend was no help, preferring the pub and his mates to fatherhood.

Her social worker tried to help her as much as possible but with a heavy case load of other needy people, she was limited in what she could do. Especially, she was not there in the night. For six months Polly struggled to cope. There were two other women on the same landing: one of whom kept complaining about the baby crying and the other who did talk to her and the children but was drunk most evenings.

She met one of her friends from the children's home while she was out shopping, "We're having a party tomorrow. Why don't you come? It will be fun and give you a bit of a break." Polly was by this time desperate to get out and it was just going to be a couple of hours.

The woman next door promised to keep an eye out for the children and Polly went to the party. The children were both asleep when she left and all seemed to be OK. It was only two hours and she had a lovely time and she did have a drink.

When she got back to the flat, all hell had been let loose. The children were screaming and so was the woman who always complained and the police were there. The woman who had promised to look out for the kids was nowhere to be found. Polly was found guilty of neglect and sent to the hostel while her children were put into care. She was totally confused and desolate by what had happened. She said several times, "But I love my kids, why can't they understand that."

We spoke many times until I was able to get her transferred to a hostel in Liverpool where she could have contact with her children and work to be reunited with them. Although she had a new officer, she still wrote to me.

Then the miracle happened as she met a widower who was twice her age and with four children of his own. She went to live with him and married him after four months. It was not long before the children were staying with her full time again.

Polly continued to write to me with news of her new family and it was clear that she was happier than she had ever been. But happiness would not last long as she was diagnosed with cancer and we lost contact.

Sugar Daddy

Jenny was a prostitute and survived by taking downers as her drug of choice was called. She lived with her boyfriend/ponce, Karl and her story was one of the weirdest I ever dealt with. To start with she had stolen a mirror from a local cinema by unscrewing it from the wall with her nail file. Why? Because it made her look thinner. In her late thirties and with her life style, she was indeed showing signs of a careless way of living. Karl was arrested with the mirror when he tried to sell it. They were both referred to me for reports.

Superficially, it did not seem to need much deep work. She had no intention of changing her life and it wasn't harming anyone but herself. His part was low-level stuff and there was no previous offending that we knew of but he had only come from Zimbabwe recently.

How wrong you can be? By the time the case was closed, I had attempted murder, armed robbery, pornography, child abuse and police corruption to add to stealing a faulty mirror. And to add to this was Albert, Jenny's sugar daddy, seventy-seven years old and a member of the Magic Circle.

It was a casual comment by Jenny that blew it all out. I asked her what was worrying her, as she was very reticent about answering, "I get worried in bed because he's a bit rough and don't like him keeping his gun under the bed. It's always loaded and I don't want it going off when we are – moving around." I told her that I would have to report this to the police. "Yes," she replied, "I don't want it there and I don't want him to get tied in with the robbery his friends are planning."

After she had gone, I contacted her arresting officer and asked him if he had searched the flat for other stolen goods.

They hadn't. "I think it would be a good idea, especially under the bed." That evening the police came to her flat with a search warrant. Karl was there and tried to stop them coming in but they did and the gun was where she had said. Karl had run away when they started the search.

Two evenings later, Jenny was viciously attacked on Tooting Bec and left for dead. She was in hospital for three days and as she was unable to return to her flat, she turned to Albert for help.

Certainly, Albert was one of her regular 'clients' but he had a genuine liking for Jenny. As he described their relationship, "We don't do much, just talk. It's nice to have someone younger to talk to and she's such a nice girl really."

Karl was soon arrested and remanded in custody to Brixton where I went to interview him. He really was the most unlikeable person I have ever met and he didn't seem to think much of me either as he threatened to kill me when he got out.

When the trial came to court, Jenny was given a conditional discharge.

Once she had begun to talk, she told the police about a paedophile ring that she had been involved with.

The result opened up a proverbial can of worms which resulted in a police raid. There were few prosecutions though there were some resignations in both public office and the police force itself. Jenny had always said that Karl had a friend in the police.

Karl however received a three-year prison sentence with a deportation order at the end. I was rather glad of that because I did think he would be a danger to me in the future.

Jenny however became the target of intimidation and felt forced to move away from South London. She soon found a new 'boyfriend' and continued to work as a prostitute and to take drugs so it was no surprise when six months later, Albert came to see me to say that Jenny was dead. One drug overdose too many.

Hercules

My main form of transport was by my bicycle. It was a 'Hercules' make so that is what I called it. It was not exactly an antique but it was getting close. It did have three gears but as the chain fell off if I pedalled backwards, they were not reliable so I stuck to one speed.

I soon learned that no self-respecting youngster would be seen dead on my bike so it was always quite safe when I visited the estates of Lambeth. The pump and lights however were fair game and I soon learned to remove them whenever I stopped. The day my lock was stolen and the bike left behind said a lot.

But someone was desperate enough to steal it. I really could not understand how anyone would want a bike as old as my Hercules and to do so at the top of Brixton Hill which had such deep-set drain covers that cycling down there was almost suicidal. The jolt of going over one would certainly have shaken the chain off. It had been OK for me, we were old friends but it was true that had it been a horse, Hercules would certainly have been in the knacker's yard so maybe the thief did me a favour. After all, the South Circular Road was not the safest road for a bike!

Strangely, my new bike nearly killed me after just a month when my toe caught the front mudguard and jammed the wheel very suddenly. Thankfully, nothing else was around at the time to hear my comments and my bruises soon mended.

Them!

Tony was on probation, and seemed to be exhibiting early symptoms of schizophrenia with paranoia at home and 'being' in a secret society which told him to do strange things.

He had been caught with a dangerous knife on Tooting Bec Common and said it was to protect himself from them. He could not say who 'them' was but they manifested themselves in voices. The police arrested him because of the danger to others and to himself. The Court sent him to Ashford Remand Centre to be assessed by a psychiatrist.

He was declared to be 'sane', responsible for his actions and fit for any form of disposal the court may wish.' He was put on probation and it was swiftly clear that his condition was not normal. He refused to eat any food at home because he believed his mother was trying to kill him and he was posting all his money in obedience to his voices to a secret organisation.

Understandably, his mother could not understand or accept this and told him to leave. I was able to find a place for him at a reasonably local YMCA but had to transfer his order as he was now out of my jurisdiction.

By now though, he had begun to relate to me as I accepted his condition and let him talk about it without threatening him. Notably, the secret society that was dominating him, became dedicated to doing good which I felt was a form of transference to me.

He settled reasonably well at the YMCA and they made sure his money was paid to them so they had his rent and food covered. Sadly, he took a bicycle from the area and though his new officer told the court of his condition, the psychiatric report again said he was fit for disposal and he was sentenced to three months detention centre. Two weeks later, he had a complete psychotic break down and had to be moved to a secure hospital.

Arthur

Arthur was in his fifties and his case was different as he was already a registered schizophrenic but he did not always remember to take his medication and then he became very forgetful and aggressive. He also became delusional and was haunted by a red devil at night-time, making it hard for him to sleep and terrifying him. The devil always endorsed the worst things that Arthur thought about himself and made him terrified of going out.

On his medication, he was reasonably 'normal', though he was scared of interviews and therefore helping him to find work was an important step in his treatment.

About this time, he became involved with a Christian healing group which performed a form of exorcism with him. It had the effect of cheering him up considerably, so much that he actually went to an interview and got a job in a warehouse. What had made the difference? He still saw the devil but he could no longer hear it. I left the area soon after that but he was still working and taking his tablets.

Holloway – 1970 and on the Move to Prison

It might have been the loss of my bicycle that unsettled me.

I had been at Tierney Road for three and a half years when the opportunity to work as a welfare officer in Holloway Prison was offered to me. I took it and once again had a steep learning curve to face. This was the Holloway of 1971, the old prison built on the model of Warwick Castle. The nearest description I can give of it is that the wing system was the same as that used on the television programme Porridge. There were two landings with about a hundred prisoners in at any one time.

My job as the welfare officer was primarily to see to any issues that might disrupt the well-being of the whole wing and to arrange for discharge when that had a welfare issue.

The 'Sump'

My wing was the F wing. It was for short-term prisoners and had a large number of alcohol and drug related crime sentences as well as a large population of prostitutes.

It was known as the 'sump' which on a car is where the dregs gather. I replaced the first male welfare officer ever in Holloway, who was affectionately known as Cuddly Dudley. I was definitely not built for the role. I was therefore only the third male welfare officer in Holloway.

The wing was a lost place. If they were not at work the prisoners stayed in their cells for all day apart from one hour of association each day and three at the weekends.

I began to record certain facts about them and after I had over a hundred case studies, fifty per cent were homeless at the time of sentence and two thirds were on prescribed drugs.

The prostitutes seemed the most normal but they too used drugs 'recreationally' and showed many signs of very low self-esteem. Almost all were working for someone sometimes called their 'protector' but commonly known as a ponce.

Slowly, we changed the ethos of the wing as a new wing governor was appointed. She was working to retirement and wanted to see things change for the better. By the time I left, she had worked to having evening association every day and a much more relaxed attitude which resulted in a similar effect on the prisoners. We tried some group work but as there were so many very short sentences it was not really viable.

With the help of the local area probation service, I was able to recruit a small group of volunteers to come in once a month just to mingle with the prisoners.

They began on February the 14th and so became the Valentines. They were instantly popular and highly respected by the inmates (See the Valentines).

The alcoholics would say things like, 'Keep my cell warm for me,' and many of the prostitutes looked on it as a welcome break. But there were others whose mental health was very worrying, and who really should not have been in prison. Several times during my time there, inmates injured themselves, often by cutting their arms. One of them told me she was trying to bleed the evil out of her. Their 'cry for help' was always there and my job was often busy with applications for news from their family and of their children.

As I commented earlier, the survey that I carried out showed that 70% of those I considered had a depressive condition for which they received prescribed medication and half had been effectively homeless at the time of conviction. Some declared that the wing was kept well behaved by lithium and valium. It seemed that the short sentence was often given when the courts did not know what to do. Most of them were what might now be called 'social casualties' for whom prison became a sanctuary.

As I commented in my introduction, the wing was very similar to the prison shown in 'Porridge' with two landings. When the 'new' Holloway was built, it became more like a hospital and was much more difficult to control, but it looked 'nicer'.

The Women

Most of the prostitutes came from London and Birmingham. It was not unusual in those areas then for the police to let them police themselves and to act only when someone else intruded into the area.

It was most notable in a well-known seaside town where only one woman came to Holloway from there, though there was an active community of prostitutes working there. It was in the summer and her 'protector' sent her there for the holiday trade but she was always arrested as she was made unwelcome by the resident group. The following short tales are just a touch of the sad world that I worked in for just over two years.

Rosie

Rosie had been a prostitute but she was now too old for a protector to use and she had effectively been dumped. With two young children, she had no support from their father. When she needed extra cash, she returned to the streets but without the protection, she was quickly taken out. When I saw her prior to release she was full of how she wasn't ever going to do it again. Three months later she was in a group of new admissions passing my office/cell door. She saw me and said, "I'm sorry, Mr Ferguson! I didn't want to but I had no money for the baby's nappy wash."

Elsie

Because mental ill health was so common, the wing doctor was always busy and we often discussed how we might deal with a particular inmate. Probably, the most damaged woman there was Elsie. When the officer opened her cell in the morning she would quickly step back as inevitably the contents of her pot would fly through the door. Plumbing in the cells was yet to be developed and slopping out was still a morning activity, but fortunately only Elsie did so this way. She rarely spoke to anyone and when she did come out of her cell she was carefully avoided by everyone. They were all grateful when she was transferred to the hospital wing.

Sally and the Chaplain

The prison Chaplain was another contact that I spoke with in some cases and he was instrumental in getting special visits especially when there was bad news from home but on this occasion, we dealt with a young woman with some lateral thinking.

In this case, Sally had vivid dreams of a dark woman threatening her every night; she even had a mark on her neck which did look like a knife mark when she woke screaming in the night. There was no knife in her cell. The Chaplain agreed to pray over her and the effect was quite dramatic as she slept well every night until her discharge and had no more evil dreams. It seems that unorthodox methods may not be a cure but they can modify the symptoms.

Myra Hindley

It is always amusing to see how people react when I say I was in Holloway Prison and even now I will be asked if I knew Myra Hindley. The answer is yes, she was in the prison while I was there but I had nothing to do with her care.

I was there when she was being considered for parole and the governor took her for a walk outside. It was not unusual to do this for long-term prisoners as they had lost the concept of traffic. One of the staff very unkindly notified the Daily Mail and this resulted in the vilification of the governor.

Right or wrong, the press coverage was vile and totally unjustified. The refusal of parole that followed led directly to a botched attempt to escape and she did for a very short spell come to F wing.

I gathered from those who did know her that she was very manipulative and this was shown in her 'escape' bid as she was aided by a released prisoner and a prison officer.

Eve

Eve was on a life sentence having killed someone in a pub fight when she was seventeen. She was still illiterate after being in the prison for twelve years. She had been released on parole but soon found she could not cope with the world and so began drinking again. She once again got into a fight, though nobody was harmed this time, but it was a breach of her parole and she was now back in prison, technically for the rest of her life.

Mary

The education department worked well on long-term wings as they had tried to do with Eve but with such short sentences it was impossible to help the great number, who were unable to read. It must be even more difficult now as the number of prisoners without English as their first language has grown considerably.

Mary was a long time visitor to Holloway as was her husband to Wormwood Scrubs. All their offending was alcohol fuelled. Neither of them was able to read so when she was due for discharge to meet him at Kings Cross Station, I was asked to escort her there to ensure they met.

It was only a bus journey of about two miles but I was very conscious of passing at least half a dozen billboard adverts for alcohol. Even I felt thirsty by the time we got there. Needless to say, they met by the bar at the station. At least they both had their tickets home.

Keep My Cell for Me

Alcohol was a major factor in the short-term prisoners though in prison they seemed to be very content. Some of them were such frequent visitors that they would have their own cell even asking the staff to keep their place. For them, prison was freedom and society a prison. As an example of them I have selected two to reflect the world in which they lived.

Alcoholic

The old woman on the down escalator at 9 o'clock in the morning ,swearing and cursing so much that everyone was keeping as far away from her as possible. Could this harridan really be the mild Olive that I had wished well to, just yesterday, "That's all right luv, just keep my cell warm for me while I'm out."

Olive had been bombed during the war and given a drink of whisky to help her nerves. Her husband had already been killed and she was on her own. The kind soul who had given her that helpful drink could hardly have realised she would twenty-five years later, be totally dependent except when she was in prison. Then she was the quiet soul grateful for the peace and security of her cell.

The same applied to others, like Geraldine. She had owned a small hotel with her husband. Her drinking had led to the loss of the business, separation and homelessness.

Serious illness followed and life in hostels and refuge centres and the street where of course she was arrested.

Prison was the only place that kept her alive. Not surprisingly, she was a very depressed lady and dreaded her release. So many of the alcoholics found their freedom and happiness in prison and hell was in the community.

At the Door

It was not unusual to be told horrific stories the night before discharge by people who may not ever see you again and very often abuse was at the root of the story. It is difficult to realise how so many become dependent on the abuser, just as prostitutes become dependent on their ponce, or how the abuse can be seen as a perverted sign of love. 'He wouldn't hit me unless he loved me' was something I heard more than once.

Yvonne was so quiet and well behaved that she was leaving almost before I knew she was there, so it was at her discharge interview that she told her story of how she had been abused by her father and then by her brothers who then used her by hiring her out to their friends.

One of the friends then took her under his protection and she was going back to him because although she was still prostituting for him, he was protecting her and she felt that he cared about her. Then, she was gone, effectively making me powerless to do anything about it. She was not the only young woman that I would meet there whose sexual experiences had begun in the home.

Miriam

Miriam was in prison for two weeks following a drunk and disorderly charge. A large shambling woman in her fifties, she had a very large family all of whom were grown up and away from home. She was now on her own as her husband had left her some time ago.

She actually seemed incoherent while she was at the prison and the Wing doctor was greatly worried by her appearance but with only two weeks he was unable to do anything.

As he expected, she returned three months later even more incoherent and shambling. His findings were quickly checked and his reference to the local doctor was for her to be referred for Huntingdon's Chorea, a rare and untreatable condition which always ends in death.

Even more awful, was that it is an inherited condition which she would have passed on to about half of her children. It is marked by people becoming less able to walk or talk normally and to be more irritable. Her illness gave all the same signs as being drunk and disorderly.

At least, she could now be treated in the community for her condition though her life expectancy was not long.

Tea at Lyons Corner House

Grace was a bit different to the other alcoholics. Married to a wealthy businessman, she had to lead an active social life. Drinking was part of that life. When he died suddenly, it became her solace but it also became an embarrassment for his family. They arranged for her to return to Kensington, which is where she had come from, and paid the rent on a pleasant flat, with a small income to sustain her. It was never enough to sustain her alcohol costs and by the end of the first week she would be found lying in the street and prison became her main home.

I saw her on one occasion in a Lyons Coffee House in Chelsea sitting in a corner with a cup of tea. I asked one of the staff if she came there often.

"Yes," they said, "She comes here in the mornings and only ever has one cup of tea, but she goes away every now and then." That was true. I bought her another cup of tea. She thanked me but I doubt if she recognised me.

I knew that she tended to come in for longer spells especially just before Christmas. I was told that she caused criminal damage and assaulted the police by throwing an empty bottle through the biggest window she could find, then running away towards the policeman, hitting him to make sure she would get long enough in prison for Christmas!

The Electric Fire

Rose and her husband were both drinkers but he would become violent and attack her, which just made her drink more. She began to receive treatment for her alcoholism and slowly made improvements. Her own anger began to express itself and she began to despise her husband for his behaviour. Everybody in the pub heard her say she would kill him if he ever hit her again.

It was a cold night when he came home and hit her again. When he had gone to bed she went to a nearby garage and bought a can of petrol.

In court, she pleaded that all she meant to do was to douse him in the petrol and threaten to set it alight if he ever attacked her again.

That is what she did. She said she had not known the electric fire was on next to the bed. She made no attempt to put the fire out. Her barrister said she was in shock when she walked out of the house and half a mile up the road to ring for the fire brigade and ambulance.

The jury found her not guilty of murder but guilty of manslaughter and she received a seven-year prison sentence from the judge who, in giving her the benefit of doubt, commented on her apparently complete lack of remorse.

Did she or didn't she? It was lucky her fellow prisoners were not on the jury.

Bad Dreams and Blue Blobs

So many of those I saw were involved with drugs. Lesley was in prison for three months after attacking six police officers causing three of them to need medical attention. She was a slight five-footer and it did not seem possibly for her to have caused such carnage. Unusually, I had to ask her what she had done. She went quiet for a while. "I'm sorry but it's quite embarrassing really and couldn't tell them in court and you are going to think it's very silly."

"Go on. I'm listening."

"Well the truth is, I was high on drugs and all I could see was big blue blobs trying to swallow me so I was lashing out at them to save myself, but I couldn't say that to a magistrate, could I?"

I had to agree with her.

Helen

Helen was an attractive and intelligent young woman who had such a low opinion of herself that she had effectively been sent to prison to save her life. She had been adopted as a baby but then rejected by the adoptive parent when she was three. A series of foster care placements did nothing to help her establish a relationship of any meaning. When she became a teenager she was a natural victim for those who target vulnerable children.

Used and abused by short term and uncaring partnerships, she had drifted into addiction very easily.

Forgetfulness was a welcome ally and when she could not forget or feel any sense of future she was prone to suicidal attempts. In prison, she was able to come off the physical addiction but she became a self-harmer and constantly at risk. We did however have a discharge plan for her with a hostel placement that could at least give her some security as she was physically clean of the drugs.

She expressed a degree of keenness until the night before her discharge when she asked to see me.

"I'm not going to be able to do it. I am sorry but I have been dreaming of needles all week and I know that I will have to inject when I get out." It wasn't the drugs that attracted her but the pain of the injection.

She was no good, nobody loved her, she deserved to be punished. I was not going to be there when she was discharged and she would have to face the demons on her own.

Sometimes, all I could was to weep at the terrible absence of hope in what otherwise could have been a good life.

Kerry

Kerry was a drug addict and intended to carry on being such when she was released. She left prison on a Friday, looking forward to her first fix. Three weeks later, she was dead, being found in a lift with a rusty needle in her groin as it was the only part of her body she could still use.

Let Me In!

Sybil or Sibbie, as she preferred, was a middle aged and poorly educated woman who had been married for twenty years to a man who totally dominated her life.

Classic of their relationship was when they went shopping, he would buy everything and pay for it, leaving her to carry it all. She was not given any housekeeping money and she had no personal freedom at all. In her simplicity, she thought that was what life was. She worked in the house as he demanded. They had no children.

Then tragedy struck, and in a rather bizarre manner, when her husband was found dead in the local cemetery stretched out on a gravestone. There was no suspicion of foul play, he had simply felt tired and lain down and died.

Sibbie was now on her own, and carried on doing what she had always been told to do, except she had never handled money.

She did the shopping and walked out without paying as she had always done. None of the agencies seemed able to help her as she was always someone else's problem. Eventually, after her fourth or fifth court appearance in as many weeks, she was sent to Holloway for a short sentence.

No doubt the court thought that this might shock her out of her behaviour as they would have already tried everything else.

Once she found her feet there, she loved it. She had all the discipline of her husband and still had no responsibility. The older prisoners looked after her, recognising her vulnerability.

She had a little job to do in the kitchens and she really did love being there. I was about to leave the prison and was very concerned about her future as because she had a home to go to, she was regarded as self-supporting. The most I could do was to alert Social Services.

I discovered later that the meek little woman had fought with the prison officers who were trying to get her to leave and spent an hour banging on the door shouting, "Let me in, let me in!"

We tend to look on the world as either good or bad but the truth is far more diverse than such simplicity. Right and wrong seem much more complex when you try standing in someone else's shoes. Sibbie couldn't go home because she did not know how to get there from the prison, so she did what she knew would work and went shopping.

Keep the Door Open

I interviewed people in a cell on the wing and for the sake of privacy, would close the door unless they wanted it to be open. I was safe because, as one of the warders said, "You're like the community stairs, everyone uses you but nobody has you to themselves."

Most of the prostitutes in the prison had depressive conditions that made them easy victims to domination by the 'ponce'. Most of them covered this up by social drug use but there was one young woman who was quite different. She enjoyed chatting to me but even her friends said, "Keep the door open." Her promiscuity was open and she admitted she enjoyed her work.

"Just ask my friends," she had said and I did.

"Oh!" said her friend, "She is awful. I mean, we were at a party last month when she comes up to me and says 'hang on to my drink, luv, I'm just popping out to do a couple.' I mean to say, she's not normal."

One day, just before she was due to go home she asked to see me. As advised, I left the door open. Not that I would have done anything but allegations were difficult to disprove.

"Why don't you close the door?" she said.

"Why?" I asked.

"I could do with a bit of practise before I get out," I kept the door wide open. That was definitely not in my job description.

Not Good Enough

Of all the young women that I worked with in Holloway, there is one in particular that I still think of. Chloe was twenty and a bright woman who had a good school record and achievement in spite of having been introduced to prostitution when she was only fourteen, by her mother. Mother was a long-time sex worker and did not even think that her daughter was being abused.

Chloe could really do well if only she could break away from her mother's influence. We found a chance for her. A new start in a job that would train her and provide accommodation. She was delighted. The plans went well and everything was in place until the night before she was to be discharged. She came to see me and I knew something was wrong straight away as she had obviously been crying.

"I'm so sorry Mr Ferguson, I can't do it. I have to go back to my mum, she needs me. I'm not good enough. Give it to someone who deserves it."

She wouldn't stay to talk but ran back to her cell. How could I tell her she did deserve it? How could I break the bond between mother and daughter even though it was corrupt? After nearly fifty years, I still don't know. I could only hope that I had planted a seed of hope that one day would enable her to make the break. You can never live anyone's life for them, however bad it might be, but I can still see her there weeping; I still feel the sadness and the grief.

Hitting the Wall

Carol was a problem for the prison because she never accepted their control. Originally sentenced to eighteen months in prison, she had been given an additional six months for assaulting on of the prison officers in an escape attempt. Normally, she would have one-third remission on her sentence if she had met the conditions. When I met her she had been in the prison for 23 months. She only had one month left of her remission.

Although, I could not condone her behaviour, I did have a touch of admiration for her spirit. I think she recognised that for she did begin talking to me. It began when I arranged to take her out of the prison to a local hostel where she could see her son who was three that day. I was advised by more than one person to keep an eye on her at all times.

As we were on the way, she asked, "What would you do if just ran away?"

I smiled and replied "I would just stand here and shout 'stop, thief' at the top of my voice."

She looked at me for a while and then said, "You would, wouldn't you! So I suppose I'd better not do it."

We had a very good meeting with her sister and the little boy but she still tried to smuggle a packet of cigarettes back under her wig. ("Sorry Mr Ferguson, but you do have to try, don't you?")

Her anger still erupted too quickly and she was down to three weeks of remission. I encouraged her to think of different ways of expressing her anger other than hitting the prison staff. In particular, I suggested she hit the wall instead.

A week later, she was in front of the governor again and was obviously getting irate. Suddenly, she went over to the wall and began to pound on it. The governor shouted, "Stop that Carol. Stop being so childish."

Carol stopped and then told the governor. "I'm only doing what Mr Ferguson told me. It was you I really wanted to hit."

Two weeks left of her emission but she was given permission to go home for a week in order to prepare for discharge. I had supported her application even though, I agreed with those who said she would never come back. Sure enough she did not come back as planned but two days later she came of her own volition.

One week left, "Sorry to let you down Mr Ferguson but I had to sort something else out."

I tried not to smile, "You did just what I expected Carol, but did you get everything sorted for your release, and do you think you will be all right when you get home."

"Yes!" she said, "And I really do not want to come back here again." Three days left and she left. I am glad to say that I did not hear anything of her again.

Valentines

As I have already said, F wing in the old Holloway was for short-term prisoners and was tough. There was no real recreation time apart from one hour at teatime.

Things though, were ready to change and a more experienced governor was appointed to the wing. She shared a lot of my thinking and soon introduced a more relaxed attitude and more association time. The group work was not a good idea as most of the women were there for very short periods of time. When my senior suggested we might try a group of volunteers, I was quick to take up the offer and soon arranged a monthly visit of volunteers.

A group of six was carefully selected and made aware of the type of prisoner they would be meeting before starting. Their role was simple – to be there and to listen. They began officially on the 14th February so instantly became known as the Valentines. They became a great success especially when one of them brought Alvin Stardust (the singer and as he was called then) for one evening.

I remember that the big song at that time was Roberta Flack singing, '*Killing me softly with his song*'. It seemed to speak to so many of them. With the coming of the Valentines, the whole atmosphere of the wing seemed to change. The prisoners were no longer just people who had been dumped but they could talk to real people and be thought of as real people themselves.

Even though it was only once a month, the Valentines were very precious.

The value of their coming was expressed one evening when I returned to the wing after seeing them out of the prison. A lot of screaming and splashing was followed by a fairly new inmate running down the landing soaking wet and going to hide in her cell.

A lot of the discipline on the wing was due to the work of the trustees, usually given the job of wing cleaner. In this case, two of the 'trustees' had 'disciplined' the new girl.

I sat in on the interview that the governor had with the two women. When she asked what their behaviour was all about their answer showed how truly valued the Valentines were.

"Well Miss, she was cadging cigarettes from the Valentines and we don't do that with them because they are our friends. They give their time to us and never ask for anything in return so we respect them and we don't ask them for cigarettes. She did and now she knows better."

Cigarettes are like 'gold dust' in the prison. The Valentines were even more precious. They continued long after I had gone and their introduction was one of the most rewarding bits of work I did in the two and a half years I was there.

The Campaign

While I was there, I became more involved with the National Association of Probation Officers and actually served on the National Professional Committee. In relation to my work, I had become very concerned by the fact that children of fourteen were being remanded to the prison, even though they were too young for any sentence to take them there. The hospital wing which is where they were held was fraught with dangers for vulnerable youngsters.

My resolution at our National conference about this was seized upon by the press and ultimately resulted in an all-party agreement in Parliament, banning the practise of under sixteen year olds being remanded to an adult prison.

A further opportunity came as I was a member of the Howard League and was invited to join a working party looking at the 'Street Offences Act.'

Our proposal for the Act to be repealed and replaced with an Act relating to nuisance, which for prostitution would apply equally to men, sadly never saw the light of day.

But it was time to move again and this time it was to my home patch, Battersea.

Battersea

It was time for me to move on and I joined the team working in Battersea, my own home patch. It had many of the same problems as Brixton but the pressure was less intense. Poverty and poor housing especially in the tower blocks were the most depressing elements of the work. I became more involved in local issues such as the Housing Association and the legal aid centre at the time when national concern had been aroused by the television programme 'Cathy come home.'

My office was just off Lavender hill, next to the courts and the police station. Clapham Junction was at the bottom of the hill. The area was, as in Brixton, gang oriented and one of my probationers was quite scared to come and see me because he had to cross a border controlled by a rival group. He was happy enough for me to visit which was easy as I walked past his house each day.

Being next to the police station was also a bit unnerving for some of the lads but I knew the area well. There was a good probation team there, similar in size to Streatham but also quite young. After six years, I was now the most experienced officer which also meant I was allocated some of the more difficult cases.

It was also when I had recently completed a course in Human Social Functioning, a psychologically based method of working which I found remarkably useful in some cases, some of which I have commented on in my case studies.

The Chairs

In my office, there was a fairly large desk, my chair and three other chairs. My desk was away from the door and filling the opposite corner. Most people came and sat in the chair which was at the corner of my desk so I only needed to move across to talk to them. One was at the open end and so directly facing me. One of them was across my desk by the window. This was my 'I-have-done-something-wrong chair'. The vast majority sat in the first two chairs.

Eddie usually sat there as well but this day he walked straight in and sat in the third chair. "What's wrong?" I asked.

He glowered at me, "What have you heard?"

"Nothing," I replied, "But you are sitting in the wrong chair and that makes me think that something has happened to upset you."

Eddie was a big black young man from Jamaica. Like so many of his fellows, he had been left at home in Jamaica when his parents came to this country in the late 1950s.

He had been raised by his grandmother and then been sent to join his parents before he was old enough to have to pay full fare. The story was only too common at this time. He had been in trouble several times for violence and was currently on a borstal licence which meant he had to report to a probation officer.

He had actually been doing very well, was working and had a steady girlfriend. But now something was wrong. He bowed his head as he spoke, clearly ashamed and worried at what he had to tell me.

He told me that his girlfriend was pregnant and wanted to have an abortion but they couldn't afford to pay for one so he had tried to forge his post office savings book and been caught. He was due in court next week.

After telling me, he sat in silence for some time looking past me and far away. I gently said to him, "Sometimes Eddie, I think you would love to be back home with your Gran, so she can hug you to try and make you feel better."

He continued to sit there quietly but a large tear ran down his cheek. I told him that I would write a report telling the court how well he had been getting on.

I did so, but the court could only see the big young man with a bad criminal record. He was sentenced to three months in prison. He moved away when he was released. His mother didn't want him there anymore so he went to stay with friends in North London. The prison sentence confirmed him in his criminal behaviour. The friend he went to stay with saw to that. Two years later, I read about his involvement with a major crime. If only they had seen the Eddie I had seen they might have let him be.

The Flannel

Elroy was another victim of the confusion at the time for young black men. He too had lived with his gran in Jamaica for many years. One day she took him to look at the aeroplanes. "Would you like to fly in one?" she asked.

Needless to say, a young boy would say yes to such an exciting adventure. When he landed, it was at Heathrow and the mother he barely knew was there to meet him. With no preparation or understanding of what had happened, Elroy was totally unable to accept what had happened. His parents were separated and he began to shuttle between them and to feel totally rejected. He had great difficulty settling at school and couldn't grasp the difference of his easy-going small school in Jamaica with the large secondary school in Battersea.

When he was put on probation we became a focus for his life. I could tell him what he should do and not do. I guided him through his applications for unemployment and housing when he did find somewhere to be independent. He liked coming in to talk with our secretaries because they didn't scare him. I listened to him. Everywhere else was a threat, a danger, a place of rejection.

His anxiety showed by heavy sweating and thus smelling rather unhygienic. Getting him through a year of probation was not too difficult because he needed so much support that our main problem was in being able to meet his needs. In the end though, he completed his time and at the same time moved into the Brixton area.

I knew that we would hear of him again because he was so anxious and explosive when he felt insecure. He really was on the cusp of social inadequacy and mental breakdown.

Sure enough, a year later, which was much longer than I had expected, he was in trouble again when his landlord evicted him and ended up in hospital as a result of Elroy's anger.

He was remanded to a probation hostel in the area, an event that I would not have recommended but with no accommodation it was the best the Court could do without sending him to prison.

That may have been better for his behaviour was becoming less and less controllable. A fight broke out in the hostel and Elroy was involved. One of the staff intervened and told Elroy to get out. My worst fears came to be as Elroy reacted angrily and struck out with almost tragic consequences.

He was remanded in custody for grievous bodily harm and sent to prison for two years. I never discovered what happened to him after that but I fear he may have become a recidivist. He would have found a place that could not reject him. His story was not isolated as so many families found that their children could not settle in this foreign land.

When Love Is Not Enough

Len and Ellen were also from the Jamaican community and they had been married for over fifteen years when it happened. The early years of their relationship had been good and they had three children. The whole family were churchgoers and Len, especially, saw his faith as integral to his life.

The three girls were all that Len could hope for; they were bright, attractive, kind and loving. But when Stella (the youngest) turned ten, it was as if Ellen became a different person. She became unsettled and argumentative. Then she began to see other men and did not hide the fact from either Len or the girls.

Len was torn between his belief in his marriage and his concern for the girls. Ellen then began to leave home for long periods making no secret of the fact she had gone to live with another man. She did not try to keep contact with Len or the girls during this time. But she also kept returning. Len with his strong belief let her return in the hope that she might change.

This time she had been away for about three months and the family had just really settled down to a routine. It was Stella's thirteenth birthday and she had some friends with her for a little party. Thankfully, it was nearly over when Ellen came in turning as she did so to blow a kiss to someone outside. She was unsteady on her feet and soon made everyone feel so uncomfortable that Stella asked her friends to leave.

Len was furious, which for a normally placid man was unusual. He and Ellen were in the kitchen shouting at each other. The children heard their father shout, "If you don't care about me you should at least think of our children."

They also heard her reply, "What makes you think that they are your children?"

Len had been carving ham for the party earlier and it was on the table in front of him. He insisted on pleading guilty to murder, even though the events became a blur in his mind.

He spent eight years in prison before release on license. His family and his friends were all waiting for him. The church that he had been so committed to had cared for his children while he was away and although they could not condone what he had done, few of them would condemn him. Len had struggled hard to retain his faith because of the great sense of guilt that he carried. He was a broken man with bad dreams.

Len knew that God still loved him and the church showed that in the way they welcomed him back, but it would be a long time before he could forgive himself.

Murder Will Always Be a Bad Dream

Causing the death of another person stays with you forever. Those were the words of a life licensee that I interviewed. His offence had been committed in the late 1950s when the death penalty was still available to the court. He had been sentenced to death but that had been commuted to a life sentence shortly before his execution was due to take place.

Charlie and one of his friends, had broken in to a shop and were stealing the goods there when the shop owner and his wife interrupted them. His friend fled the scene quickly and was never caught but the wife attacked Charlie with a large kitchen knife. In the ensuing struggle, the knife ended up in her, killing her.

Even though Charlie had not gone with the intention of killing, the death occurred during the commission of a crime and that merited the death sentence. He had served over fifteen years before release on parole (in his case a life license). One of the conditions of this was to report to a probation officer weekly.

He had been released to a local hostel and was actually one of a colleague's cases but as he was on holiday Charlie had to report to me.

He came in and sat down. I explained how my colleague was away. He was aware of this. He sat there quietly so I initiated the conversation. "How are you settling at the hostel?"

"It's good not to be locked up all the time."

"How long were you in prison?"

"Not long enough."

"What makes you think that?"

"I should be dead. At least in prison I knew I was being punished, but I can't get used to being free."

"Why not?"

"I can't sleep, she won't let me sleep."

"Who is she?"

"The woman I killed. I see her every night as soon as I shut my eyes I see what I did."

"What do you see?"

"There was a large mirror behind her and I saw her sliding down my body and then lying on the floor with that terrible knife in her chest."

"But you didn't go there to kill her, did you?"

"No. But I did kill her and now she won't leave me alone."

Charlie was so haunted by what he had done that six months later, he got very drunk and drowned in the river.

Like, Man!

It seemed to be Andy's favourite sentence and it really became quite tedious listening to him bemoaning his lot in life, punctuated by the word 'like' so I decided to let him hear himself. I recorded some of our conversation then played it back to him. The result was electrifying.

"That's not me!"

"Oh yes it is," I replied

He sat back in his chair, speechless for a while. "That's like – awful! What can I do?"

These are the magic words for any probation officer. They are ready for a change, and begin to work on that change.

Andy was in a mess. Not only did he sound like a discarded hippy but he was acting like one. He was out of work, his girlfriend had chucked him out, and wouldn't let him see either her or their child until he showed that he was willing to make an effort to support them. He was sleeping on the floor of a friend's room but that was not going to last. In desperation, he had stolen food from a supermarket.

"What do you think you need to do?" I asked.

"I don't know like. I sound so pathetic. What can I do like?"

"How about getting some work?"

"I tried but what can I do like?"

"I think you know what to do. Just go to the employment exchange and take the first job they offer. It doesn't matter what it is. Then come back next week and tell me what you did."

I added, "By the way, when you go for an interview don't keep saying 'like', that is one of the things that sounds pathetic and you don't want that anymore."

Andy went as suggested and was given a job sorting out coat hangers out at a store in London. He was working in the warehouse. Because he had found a job he was able to get a starter payment from the Exchange and had rented a room in Battersea with it. He walked to work to save money and made his own sandwiches to avoid the cost of London shops.

Two weeks later, he came late to see me and apologised for missing the previous week. The reason was that the warehouse boss had asked him to be his deputy (there were only three of them). The next time I saw him, his boss was off sick and he was in charge and coping with it.

His self-confidence went up dramatically and before long he was back with his girlfriend and daughter. He was so transformed that I couldn't understand how he could have got into such a state as before.

When I saw him for the last time, he had been placed on a management training scheme by the store. He said he just needed someone to believe in him and thanked me for setting him in the right direction and not once did he say 'like'.

Responsibility

Brian was on probation for a minor drugs offence and because the court thought he needed to have a guiding hand. He was twenty and had been in care until he was seventeen since when he had drifted.

In the last year, he had become involved with Carol, a woman nearly ten years older who was widowed and had three young children. She was a strong-willed woman struggling to raise her children in sub-standard accommodation on the eighth floor of a block of Council flats.

They seemed to give each other mutual support and obviously cared a great deal about each other. Brian told me that being responsible for someone made him feel good.

It wasn't easy especially when they woke up one night with the youngest screaming. When they put the light on they found the wall was crawling with bugs. The bed and everything in there had to be incinerated and the room vacated until it could be deloused. As a priority, it only took three months but they coped. "What else can you do?" said Carol.

Carol was a natural carer and loved her family greatly and she had fought hard to keep them all together. I think she saw in Brian another casualty of the system and in need of a mother while she needed as much emotional support as she could get.

Although Brian was unemployed and unskilled, he was good with the children and she was able to supplement their social security money with some casual cleaning work.

Then their generosity backfired on them when they took one of Brian's old friends in, while he was going through the court on drug charges. He overdosed and died during the night. To their relief, they were exonerated of any blame but it was another unwelcome hurdle in their struggle to cope.

Towards the end of his order, Brian came in to see me unexpectedly. He wanted to tell me that he had been in the public gallery of the court when he saw the Warrant Officer pointing. For the first time in his life, he knew it couldn't be for him.

Just before I moved, he found his first full time job on a building site. The money was good, better than Social Security and Carol was happy to be clear of being dependent on the 'dole' as she called it.

Cockroaches

Working in South London in the '70s meant that I was there when the influence of the Krays and the Richardson gangs was still felt and the great train robbery had involved a lot of the local villains. Ben ran a stall in Battersea and was well into the local crime scene. The story was that he had been down to drive one of the cars in the train robbery, but a dose of flu' had put him out of action.

Vic had been found guilty of armed robbery so was away for a long time. I mention this because his wife was friendly with Ben and there were other links to major crime but Daphne was very much on the fringe especially since Vic had gone down.

She was put on probation for shoplifting, her excuse being, "I needed it but social had stopped my money." After being initially quite suspicious of me, she warmed to the fact that someone was actually there helping her, advising her on how to do things but letting her do them herself.

She was mid-forties, very strong-willed and with a colourful vocabulary especially after she had been drinking. This had not endeared her to the local agencies, in particular the housing department with whom she had a long running feud.

This had not been helped by Vic who was in considerable arrears when he was there and she had had to cope with this on her own.

She was not at all well in herself having already had a breast removed because of cancer. As a result, she was unable to work but it had not prevented her from enjoying her drink.

After the first few weeks, we began to get on well as I accepted her as she was and didn't preach to her. The dampness of her flat did not help her illness and it was no surprise when she discovered cockroaches in her kitchen.

When she complained to the housing officer about this, he had told her that she was imagining them and that she shouldn't drink so much. Fortunately, we had been talking about anger management the week beforehand as otherwise he might have regretted his words sooner.

I suggested to her that she catch one and then take it in to show him that she was not imagining them. I recall her sitting back and saying, "What a good idea." I had not expected her to collect a whole jar full or that she would tip them on to his desk with the words, "Here's my 'effing' imagination."

The whole office had to be fumigated but so was her flat.

It was only a one-year order so our contact ended quite soon but I received a Christmas card from her with a little note to say she was OK for the next four years.

Illness

Sometimes behaviour can be caused by a chemical imbalance such as the young mother I wrote a report on. It was clear she was struggling and she was constantly tired. She had walked out of a shop without paying and they had not accepted her apology. The court recognised that she might be telling the truth and asked for a report before sentencing.

When I called, she was in tears and very fearful of the court. She was so unlike anyone who would break the law as she was secure in her accommodation and was still seeing the baby's father and being supported by him, though she told me he was worried by her erratic behaviour since the baby had been born.

I used the Social Functioning Questionnaire with her and the results showed very clearly that she was a well-balanced young woman but very lacking in energy.

Having a wife who had suffered from an iron deficiency, I suggested she go to see her doctor and get a blood test done, which she did. His prescription for iron tablets soon turned her into the person she really was and the court were able to give her an absolute discharge as she had already paid for the shopping.

The next case was slightly different in that the deficiency had already been identified. This time it was a woman in her thirties who was writing a book.

She had a deadline to reach and so she could stay awake longer she had altered her prescription to get more amphetamine.

Blood tests had proved that she was in fact suffering a potassium deficiency and that the only thing the amphetamine was doing was to increase her anxiety level to the point where she could not concentrate.

Her medication was changed and she kept a supply of bananas handy, because of their high level of potassium, for when she was flagging. I am glad to say her book was completed by the deadline and she was much happier.

Beryl was a mother of four boys and she had just gone through a divorce. She coped on a very shallow level and drank at lunchtime before the children returned home. The oldest boy was used to getting the tea and was in fact acting as a carer for his mother.

It was obvious that it was not just the drinking that caused the problem as she was in fact desperately lonely and seeking inappropriate relationships. The doctors were sure that there was a medical condition but it was a long time before the diagnosis of lupus was made a condition where the virus attacks all the organs so that one by one they start to fail. She kept in contact with me when I left and her eldest son wrote to me when she died as a result of the lupus.

Transgender

Jim was on parole having been released from prison as a result of a burglary which he said was to raise the funds he needed for a transgender operation. He was genuinely on the waiting list and did eventually have the operation and became Julie. The main problem then was that if he committed any further crime he would still be sentenced as a man.

As a child, he had been dressed as a girl by his very obsessive mother who had wanted him to be female. His young adult life was apparently very confusing and he behaved as a young man, married in his twenties and had two children. At this time, he was still a cross dresser. His marriage broke down and he spent several short spells in prison, often as a result of violence. He became aware that his different sexuality was not homosexual because he wanted to be a woman. He went through all the tests that were available in those days and it was agreed that he was indeed a suitable case for transgender and not just to live as a cross dresser.

He was not, however, able to take the final steps until he had completed his parole. He actually became a cause celebre as it was still in the very early days of this being recognised as a possibility. He normally reported to me as a man but towards the end of his parole he had taken the step of living as a woman and dressing as a woman so reporting dressed as a woman. I heard later that he had successfully made the transition.

Bungled!

John was sitting on the floor outside my office when I returned from lunch. He wasn't expected so I knew something quite drastic must have happened as I normally had trouble getting him to report at all.

He slumped down in the chair and he had evidently been drinking, "My mates are looking for me. I think they want to kill me but it weren't my fault we got stuck."

Feeling as if I had come in half way through a story, I said, "Let's start at the beginning. Why are your mates looking for you?"

He went on to tell me that he had been driving the car in a smash and grab raid. He had as instructed backed the car into a jeweller's shop window. His friends grabbed what they wanted and jumped back into the car. The alarm was blaring away. As he put his foot down, nothing happened. Somehow the car had become lodged on a ridge with the back wheels off the ground.

By now, they could hear the police car coming. The mates jumped out, lifted the car off, back in and they were off but with the police in pursuit. They drove into a wood where they had a switch car.

They were nearly home when they realised that the main bag of jewels was still in the previous car. John handed himself in to the police and received two years in prison. His friends got three years. Apparently, even the judge laughed.

In the Wardrobe

I was rather surprised to be given a parole supervision on a seventy-six your old man especially when I saw it was for blackmail and assault. His story was remarkable and unusual.

George was having a relationship with a younger married woman. To all accounts, he had been very generous to her. In time, she had tired of him and started a new relationship with a retired police officer. George was understandably rather upset by this and threatened to tell her husband if she did not return some of his gifts to her.

Her new boyfriend set a meeting up with George, apparently to sort it all out, but had one of his still working colleagues there, hiding in a wardrobe. It really did sound rather like a Whitehall farce but the result was that George became angry and threatening, at which point the policeman emerged from the wardrobe and arrested him. A recording had been taken of the conversation so the blackmail charge was proved.

By itself, that might not have been enough for a longish prison sentence but they discovered that George had been abusing young teenage girls. Unbelievably, he had advertised his skills in enlarging their breasts. Even more unbelievable was that two young women had come along with their parent's consent.

The court was not amused and had sent him to prison for three years. He assured me that he had learnt his lesson.

Grass

In this case, 'grass' is a slang term for a police informant and Reg would not normally have had anything to do with it, in fact like most offenders he would have despised the person who did it. Unwittingly, I was his means of communication as one of our secretaries was married to a police officer in the CID and Reg would visit and slip his information to her so he was never seen to be in contact with the police himself.

It all began when he was released after serving three years imprisonment for burglary. As he got home, there was a note on the door saying, "Reg, I have gone and I'm not telling you where. I have looked after the children on my own for long enough and it's your turn now. They are next door and they know what is happening. Shelley."

As he was out on parole, he came to see me almost immediately as he lived just around the corner from the office. I put him in touch with Social Services and they came to see him the next day. The children were quite glad to see their father but didn't really know why their mother had gone and the Social Worker felt that with the support of the next-door neighbour and with my supervision he could be all right. To his credit, Reg did not try to duck out of his unexpected responsibility but he certainly made full use of my supervision and the next-door neighbour.

The fear of having to go back into prison and thereby losing the children gave him a strong incentive.

A minor brush with the law brought him in contact with local CID and an offer that he could not refuse.

The girls were eleven and nine at this time and were old enough to look after their own hygiene and knew how to use the washing machine, much to Reg's relief.

They looked after him as much as he looked after them.

Then Reg made a mistake and burgled a house in Surrey. There was no protection for him there and he was fortunate to get a probation order because of his children.

He was still learning how to deal with the official bodies such as the Social Security and the school but they all knew how he was trying to be responsible for the first time in his life and coped with his exasperation at the slowness of responding to his needs.

I had one example of it when I was slow in dealing with him and he stormed into the office and began shouting at me from about a foot away. I must have been having a bad day as well because I bellowed back at him and told him in simple English not to shout at me and to go away and come back the next day when he could talk properly. He turned and left the office.

Several members of our staff asked me if I was all right afterwards as my response to Reg was unlike my normal quieter way of working. Still, Reg returned the next day and we were able to sort the issue out. The time came and I was due to move to Reading. This disturbance to his support caused him considerable anxiety and he had a bad row with the head-teacher which led to a case conference being held.

For some reason, I was not involved in it but I had spoken to the social worker the day before.

I called to see him that afternoon. I knocked and the door opened slightly. Pushing it more, I called in to Reg and took a step into the house only to find him standing behind the door with an axe in his hand, raised and ready to hit. There are several situations that all the training in the world cannot prepare you for.

I looked straight at Reg, "That's not for me, is it Reg?" After making sure there was nobody else, he came down and we were able to talk and to calm him down before the social worker did come. I must admit that writing about it was far less worrying than standing there with an axe above my head.

He had thought they were coming to take the children into care. Thankfully, I was able to reassure him that the meeting had been to talk about how they could help him in his care of the children.

I also pointed out that it was just as well it was me at the door as otherwise he would have been inside and not able to look after the children. I arranged for him to come into my office to meet the officer who was going to look after his supervision when I left. I also made him promise to behave himself with her. It may sound as if I was treating him a bit as a child, but in a way he was.

His relationship with the police also helped to keep him at home but it was a very risky thing as he would have been at considerable risk if it had become known to the criminal gangs.

His new officer knew Reg already from having covered for me when I was on holiday and of all my colleagues, she had the tough qualities that are needed for supervising the more demanding client without freaking out. Even Probation officers can feel overwhelmed at times.

That's Not Me!

Alice came from a good family, a professional family but a family destroyed by alcohol. Her father had been a highly regarded doctor who committed suicide when his alcoholism became too much for him. Her mother had spent long spells in hospital because of alcohol and her brother had been killed in a car accident when he was drunk.

Alice had still done well at school but in her last year she began to take drugs. Her then boyfriend, took her to parties and clubs where drugs were freely available. Drugs helped her forget her grief and stopped her from drinking but by the time I met her she was injecting heroin and rarely able to work. She still had the security of her home but it was also the centre point of her sadness. Being arrested and put on probation was a shock to her. She didn't want to accept she had a problem even when she became seriously ill and almost died. That did however, make her value her life and so we could begin to work on motivation for the future. The drugs however did still have a control over her until one day when she was at the hospital.

She needed a fix so she nipped in to the toilets. As she was about to inject, she saw a sign on the door. "Drug addicts! Please do not fix in here as it may be used by children." She thought how terrible it was for children to be exposed to drugs and then realised that she was the problem. She had cried for ten minutes trying to say 'it's not me! It's not me!' But it was.

We began to work on a questionnaire that I used to see if that might give her a starting point. One of the questions was, 'How far do you feel you have you achieved your ambition in life.' The scoring was nought to twenty and she had nought. She realised that all her ambition was the next fix and she could not see beyond it. But she wanted to. I told her to go away and after a week to come back and tell me where she wanted to go however crazy it sounded.

The following week, she returned and she knew – *I want to be a nurse and to work with people like me who have drug and addiction problems.* She had said it before to others but they had always said it was impossible. I asked her how she was going to get there and what did she need to do.

For a year, she stayed at a clinic clearing herself from the physical addiction. It was hard time and it times very frightening for her. By now, her probation order had finished but I continued to work with her on a voluntary basis. Several times, she nearly gave up but the day came when she could come home. Target two was about to begin.

At least twelve months in a job without relapse. She got a menial job in one of the big London stores and at the end of this she was accepted for a training course in nursing. She became aware that it was not just the drugs she had to conquer but her addictive personality.

Three years later, I had a letter from her to say she was now a sister on a ward dealing with addictions.

The last time I saw her, she was spearheading a new centre for the treatment of addictions on television.

It was obviously a great help that her academic ability meant that achieving her dream was possible and it was a question of enabling her to recognise that it was possible and having a light support to get her through the two years of torture she had to endure that got her where she could be.

She was still an addict but now she could recognise that and handle it. Her achievement in doing so was a real triumph of determination as the power of addiction undermines confidence and seeks only its own ends. People cannot stop because they are told to do so, they must have motivation and a lot of courage.

I confess to a feeling of joy that I was able to help her do what she did.

Patience

Fred was put on probation for two years, mainly because the court thought that he was in danger of being led into more serious crime because of his poor school attendance and his involvement with the gang with whom he had got into trouble. He reported regularly and never got into any more trouble. I saw him in my office and visited the home several times. He was in his last year at school and it was clear that academic achievement was not his forte. Since leaving the fellowship of the gang, he tended just to stay in and watch television.

Worst of all for me was that he was almost totally monosyllabic. In two years, I cannot remember him saying anything more than yes or no but he did keep out of trouble and his order finished 'satisfactorily'.

Two years later, I was told that Fred was in the office waiting to see me. The change was almost unbelievable. He was bright eyed, keen and full of the fact that he had just passed his driving test. We talked for about half an hour about his great sense of success and how this had opened up new opportunities for him at work. Suddenly, Fred believed in himself and in the future.

He had come to tell me even before he had gone home. I learnt from him that being patient and accepting him as he was made me the only person who had not told him he was stupid and no good for anything. I had always encouraged him. It was a privilege to share in his joy and success.

Potatoes

Ken came to me on borstal license and with one of the least promising referrals I had ever seen. He had several previous offences most of which involved violence. His offence before the sentence for borstal training was for attempted murder; he had run over his victim and then reversed the car back over him. Fortunately, the injuries were not as severe as they might have been. He had only been in the borstal for the minimum time because he was so disruptive and he was definitely not keen on supervision.

I was, therefore, quite surprised when he reported on release. I outlined the conditions of his license and said that as far as I was concerned that was what I expected. He grunted and then said, "I don't want to go back inside, it does my head in!"

Why I said what I did I cannot recall because it sounds very odd now. It was however quite inspired, "I'm glad to hear that Ken. Now I've told you what I expect but if you really want to change we will have to work on this lovely anger you have."

Yes, he did look at me as if I was mad, but he asked the question, "What do you mean?"

I explained that as far as I was aware he was riddled with anger and it was no use telling him not to be angry because he was angry and he either had to learn how to control it or it would ruin his life completely.

He listened. I continued, "I want you to go now and come back next week at the same time and if you are willing, we will start to see how you can use it for good and not for bad."

He left and reported the following week as I had asked. "What can I do?" he asked.

We began to look at ways for him to use up his energy in sport and by going to the gym. Then be began to look for work that would use his energy. He found a job in a greengrocers shop and that was quite physical. He moved out of the area but I retained his supervision as by then it only had a short time to go. Then he committed a minor offence and appeared in a court outside my area. I wrote a report explaining the work we had been doing but the clincher for him was the owner of the shop who came and gave him a glowing reference.

Ken was given a conditional discharge. He had kept his anger in check for nine months. During that time, we had looked at what the root of his anger might be and it wasn't hard to find when he talked of the physical abuse he had suffered at the hand of his mother. Bereft of love and taught to be violent himself, he had never found a reason to be anything else but the victim of his uncontrolled anger.

Throughout his life experience, people had told him to stop being angry, but it was only when he came here that he was effectively given permission to be angry and then to work with it in a constructive way.

We kept in touch after the license came to an end. He married and they had a child and he found the love he had never experienced as a child. The last time I heard from Ken was in a letter to let me know that the baby was well (she had been ill for some time).

It ended with a PS:

"When it's too much for me now, I take it out on the potatoes."

Too often, we are scared by people's anger and as such we fail to see the hurt person inside the violence. By accepting Ken's anger as a reality for him and not denying it or punishing him for it, Ken became the hard working, loving father and husband, even though he still did need the potatoes.

Reading

Though I was happy in Battersea, my career needed to move up a notch and I began to apply for senior positions and this resulted in our move to Reading in 1979. At this time, there were three area teams and the work was much as I had known it. I was given the Whitley area to manage with a team of five officers. Because of the heavy workload, I still had some face-to-face work in what was seen as one of the difficult parts of Reading. The following episodes come from this period.

The challenge came when we moved to specialist appointments and in 1982 I was given the county responsibility for the supervision of juvenile offenders and for the Family Courts. Having only learnt how to drive when I reached fifty, my new driving licence came into use as I now had three office bases, Windsor, Newbury and Reading.

In Reading, we began to deal with juvenile offenders through a Joint Agency Group which effectively became a sub-judicial way of dealing with juvenile crime through the police cautioning system. I worked alongside a police inspector, senior social worker and the Education Welfare Officer. As the assessments were made soon after the offence was committed instead of three or four months later, we were able to take voluntary action and to place the responsibility back into the family after a police warning. Where something more was needed or if the youngster was already on a caution then we proceeded to court.

In the space of three years, we had reduced the number of juveniles going to court from 350 a year to just about 100. The number of custodial sentences came down from 50 to just two. Partly, this was due to the fact that we had released time and space to deal effectively with those who were in danger of further offending. The re-offending rates dropped by over a third.

I was able to assess the effects of this by getting permission to study for a master's degree at Reading University in Criminal Justice and this joint agency work was the subject of my final dissertation. Working academically with seven police officers was quite a challenge as well. Ultimately, the work was so successful that Social Services were able to take on all the juvenile work and my team took on all the Family Court work in the county.

Before we began to specialise, there were some cases with which I was involved, here are a few of them.

The Brick

The brick is one case that we were not able to deal with in this fashion as Sue insisted on pleading not guilty. Cautions could only be given if the offender confessed. Sue was a lively young girl (16) who had been charged with criminal damage, having thrown a brick through a school window. I was on court duty that day and she was insisting on pleading not guilty so the case was put back and I was asked to have a word with her.

She had been to a party at the school and as she was leaving a pupil at the school (which was a boarding school), leaned out of the window and shouted abuse at her.

She found half a brick and threw it at him. She said she didn't intend to break the window. She accepted my advice that a broken window was better than attempted murder. The court then put her on probation.

During the time on probation, she married at seventeen and had two children before the two years were up. Like so many other lively clients, I found her both challenging and likeable.

A classic example of her life was when her husband to be was attacked by a gang, she went to his defence and drove them away. She was only five-foot tall but she had a six-foot temper. I just hope her husband never upset her! She did calm down when her first baby was born and motherhood seemed to suit her well in spite of her young age.

Broken Jaw

When I saw 'John' for the first time, he had his jaw wired up as the result of being attacked in a pub car park, during which he had been robbed of what little money he had. Homeless, alcoholic, unwanted by his family and heavily in debt with a long list of fines for drink related offences, John did not know how to cope except to drink more.

Prison came as a blessing to him as it was a way of clearing his court debts and it gave him time to sober up and heal from his injuries.

'John' was a Sikh and going to prison was deeply shameful. He found it hard to accept my help, which as he was a prisoner was voluntary and not part of any order. When he realised that I was really trying to help him and not wash my hands of him, it made him make a real effort. I found a bed and breakfast place for him on his release. He joined alcoholics anonymous and got himself a job as a cleaner in a local hotel. He wanted to help and to build up his own self-respect again and so his landlord took a chance and let him become the site manager.

It was like an apprenticeship for John who determined to buy a house and to let the rooms out. This idea became an obsession with him and he saved every penny that he could.

The result was that, in little more than a year he had enough to buy a terraced house. He lived in one room and controlled the kitchen.

The other four rooms were let out to other homeless people that we had contact with. His official contact with me was by now over but he kept in contact and often invited me over to see what he had done to the house and then to the second house that he bought. He only took referrals from the Probation Service as a way of saying thanks.

He re-established contact with his sons now that he had recovered his pride and been able to achieve something with his life. He did have a brief breakdown but it actually made him realise his fragility and that he was still an alcoholic and could not drink any alcohol at all.

After two years, he bought a car. Fortunately, he had never had a car in his drinking years. He was a rather ferocious landlord and would accompany his residents to the social security to make sure he had the rent before they got to the pub. The car got bigger and a third house was bought.

When I last saw him, he stopped his car in the road to greet me and thank me for believing in him. As he drove off he leaned out of the car and said, "It's a long way from broken jaw!"

Prison broke his cycle of dependence and set him free to change his life around with just one person believing in him and his own desire to be respectable again.

Ginger

He may have only been fourteen but he was very tall for his age and had a mop of ginger hair. Stealing cars was therefore not a good idea as he was always readily identified. Like many young boys, TWOC (taking without consent) was almost addictive as it made them feel in control of their lives which otherwise were chaotic.

Changing to bicycles was certainly safer for the community but still very noticeable except now he only rode when it was dark. He became one of a group of young cycle thieves who were responsible for a mini crime wave with their stealing of bikes. Their downfall was when Ginger was seen riding a touring bike which had been stolen from a professional cyclist.

It was not long before the whole gang were in court. One of them came from a house with a large garden and a shed at the bottom of the garden which was not used. Here the bikes were kept and stripped of saleable items. Some of the bikes which could not readily be identified were being used by members of the gang. Gingers love of speed was their undoing.

They were quite professional in their disposal of the stolen parts with an advert in the local paper giving a mobile number belonging to one of the older boys. His bedroom was like a small junk shop. The parents were all astounded by what their children had been doing, especially as they too had to be in court.

A Kiss at Waitrose

Sometimes, it is later that you discover how effective your work has been and this was certainly the case with Mary

I am not often surprised by what happens but when a young woman at the other end of the aisle suddenly squealed my name and rushed up to me, grabbed me in an affectionate hug and kissed me, I was a bit nonplussed and the staff seemed quite amused.

Fortunately, I soon recognised her. Mary didn't stay long but thanked me for saving her life by giving her so much support and encouragement some fifteen years ago when she had been at the point of killing herself because her life had become so awful.

I did remember her and indeed she was a much-changed person. When she had been taken to court by Social Security for making a false claim, she was pregnant, with two small children, her husband had just gone to prison for a lengthy sentence leaving her with massive debts.

His abuse of her had led to her being cut off from all her friends and family. She was truly alone and in desperate circumstances. Just before the court case, she lost her baby.

It was soon clear to me that her husband had been making the false claims and that she was now being underpaid by the Social Security.

The court gave her a year's probation order and asked me to try and sort out the confusion with Social Security.

Although I helped by getting some early financial support and some new furniture to replace what the bailiffs had taken, most of what I did was to enable her to go to the right places and take control over her own life.

With my support she soon showed her ability to manage. It was a long and slow process but eventually Social Security accepted they were wrong and gave her the support to which she had always been due. It was not long after that housing found her more suitable accommodation.

She told me briefly that she was now at work in a refuge centre helping people who were like her.

As her order finished, we kept in touch for a while just to help with advice. Then she was away until that kiss in Waitrose.

The Long Shadow

I saw Lorna for over twenty years as she needed a long-term relationship she could believe in. Initially, she came to us by being sent to the Elizabeth Fry Hostel in Reading. They were reluctant to take her initially as she came from Nottingham area with a record of truculence and drug abuse. For some reason, I thought she was just the sort of girl that they should be helping. I was right for she desperately needed a period of stability.

It took time to get her story from her but she had suffered physical abuse from her father until her mother left for a new partner. Then as she got older, her stepfather began to sexually abuse her and so did her brother. When she ran away, she stole food and hid in the bus station. When she was arrested, she refused to go home but was scared to say why because her mother would not believe her.

She was just settling at the hostel when she was attacked and raped in Reading. The attacker was arrested and jailed but the psychological effect on her was to make her withdraw into herself to such an extent that she could not bear anyone to touch her.

She took to carrying a large knife with her and when her then probation officer tried to take it off her, she attacked him. I heard the row and went into the office to find them rolling on the floor. My colleague held the knife out to me and I took it from him. Immediately, she let him go but I left the room with the knife while my colleague tried to calm her down.

She came to my office about quarter of an hour later. We talked for a while and she told me that she always had the knife with her as it was the only way she felt safe.

Much against my better judgement, I gave the knife back to her telling her to keep it out of view.

I also took charge of her order myself as my colleague was badly shaken by the experience. The fact I had returned her knife, gave her a sense of trust in me. She knew I would keep my word.

The storms were never far away from Lorna. She overdosed on antidepressant tablets several times and although she always reported as required it was only towards the end of her order that she began to talk about her history of being abused.

About this time, NACRO set up a project for long term unemployed people and Lorna was well suited to this job. Perhaps, because my wife was working with the scheme, Lorna agreed to give it a try. It was perfect for her. She was safe and showed that she could be trusted by becoming the wages clerk for three years until the scheme was closed down due to funding being transferred. She immediately applied for and got a new job but left this as soon as she felt threatened but still found another job. She was there for three months when she was sacked and accused of stealing.

She was devastated and not guilty of the charge. Her anger vented itself on the shop window. The court was sympathetic and back on our books she came. Six months later, the supervisor who had accused her was arrested and charged for the thefts.

Sadly, Lorna was never able to work again as she returned to her drug abuse, and her distrust of everyone.

The day that Lorna gave me a hug was such a surprise because of her fear of being touched. It was the high point of her trust in me. During that last order, she often ran short of money and we had a five-pound note that went back and forward because she always paid it back. On one occasion when she seemed very down, my secretary was worried that she might do herself harm. Lorna waved the money at her – "Don't worry I have to pay my debts."

She still depended on antidepressant drugs but also went into an anorexic state wanting to deny her female sexuality.

Part of this was the abuse of Exlax chocolate. When at the age of forty she caught flu, her system was unable to cope any longer and it developed into pneumonia and she died.

We went to the funeral and watched as her cardboard coffin passed through the curtains. As she had shown in her time at NACRO, she was an intelligent and able young woman but her life was so dominated by the long shadow of her abuse that only her death would have given her peace.

The Latter Days

The move to being the County Court Welfare Officer brought a new range of challenges as I had to build my team up from scratch and find an office suitable for children.

I now had a team of six officers in three offices across the county. It was my last job in probation and the one which gave enormous satisfaction as we were able to be involved in a positive way. My team was first class.

Although I had always written reports for the County Court in divorce cases when the care of the child was in dispute, I was now charged with managing the county team and it was in some ways more fraught than criminal work and often more criminal.

I recall a few examples out of the many sad cases we had to deal with where a murder resulted. The father, in both cases, was obsessed with his 'ownership' of the family and killed them rather than lose them. There is often a fine line in such cases about the best interests of the children. Normally, it is always in the best interests of children to have good contact with both parents and they have a right to that. The parents though have a right to be parents but not to have access to the children if they are a risk to the child. Determining that is always a very fine line.

The stories of the Divorce Court are not for telling in this book as they might refer to people who could be identified but these two incidents show how close it is sometimes to say what is criminal.

Excuses

Mr H. was trying to get contact with his children but this was being wilfully refused by their mother. I was tasked with trying to find out what the children felt. They two older children both wanted to see their father but the three-year old was too young to be asked. I arranged for them to meet father in a neutral setting, but again mother refused to let the children go.

Court hearings were similarly not attended and when mother was actually summonsed to attend, she claimed that she could not come because she was breastfeeding the baby. As the baby was nearly four, her excuse was barely credible.

The only recourse the court were left with was to commit her for contempt but father was not able to offer the children a home as he had moved out of the family home when the marriage broke down and now lived in a one bedroom flat and as such he was not willing to risk the children's welfare and so withdrew his application.

No crime as such was committed but Mother's behaviour was close to being abuse, though she cared for them perfectly well on a physical level.

The second excuse matter related to a couple who had been separated for two years and Father was getting very concerned at Mother's negative influence on their son

I saw the child when he was with his father and the relationship was very good with both Father and his new partner. He wanted the child to come and live with them because he thought the mother was planning to leave the country. I arranged to visit Mother but twice my appointment was cancelled at the last minute. Eventually, I visited without an appointment. The house was empty.

I was able to contact the grandmother and discovered from her that Mother had in fact left to live in Germany with her new partner. In this case, the court issued a summons for her arrest.

The third case was again a question of the mother refusing the children's access to their father purely out of spite because he had a new partner.

I called to see her and the children. I was told that they didn't want to see me and that they were scared of me. I insisted that I should see them. Sure enough, they were hiding when I called but I saw the girl behind the settee. I said, "Boo," and she began to laugh. They had been told to hide from me.

Mother came back into the room and they sat close to her while I explained that I was not here to take them away but just to find out if they wanted to see their father. Mother quickly said, "No, they don't want to see him."

As she did so the girl, who was about eight, looked her straight in the eye and said, "That's not true, Mummy. You know we want to see Daddy."

I like eight-year olds, they seem to have no fear. But that was to Mother's credit for with all her animosity the children were quite able to be different, and yes, they did get to see Dad.

Yvonne had been 'forced' by her husband into prostitution, not an uncommon problem for prostitutes, and had escaped with her daughter when she feared that the child might become involved as well. She was in hiding and did not even let me know where she was living. Her husband applied for the custody of their child, citing her prostitution as a reason for him to have the child.

I had to contact her through her mother's Church minister and she did call in to see me and bring her daughter once she had realised that I would not tell her husband where she was. He tried to get the judge to make me reveal her address and did get a court hearing at which I was summonsed to attend. He was there with a girlfriend. I was able to assure the court that the child was being well cared for and was happy with her mother and that it would not be in the interests of either of them to have contact. The court accepted what I said but insisted that the mother should come in person.

Yvonne was terrified but when she was given an assurance that she would be protected if need be. She bravely went and told the judge what sort of life she had been subjected to. The application of the husband was refused in the best interests of the child.

The End and a New Beginning

Sadly, I became the architect of my own early retirement when we had an inspection and I just let him see how we were. The result was that we got an extra officer but my job was downgraded to half time as the extra post was to stop me from having to do some reports myself. I had always felt it important to be hands on and to show and not just tell my team what to do.

I was immensely proud of the standard of work and their dedication, and I still am. When I retired in 1994, most of them continued the work until their own retirements.

This was also a time when we developed new ideas. Mediation was sponsored by probation and based at the County Court, so I became the liaison officer on their management committee. When I retired from probation, I retrained as a mediator and worked there until at seventy, I decided to retire. I remained on the committee for a few years but age was catching up on me.

The second major development in the work of Court Welfare was the setting up of voluntary contact centres where parents who 'needed' to see their children in a safe place could do so. The same applied to children who needed a safe environment. With one enthusiastic volunteer who took on the setting up and arranged the training, we had five centres in Berkshire within two years.

Looking Back

I retrained as a family mediator but even after twenty years of retirement, I still say I was a probation officer. The work we did was valuable in several ways. It was described as to supervise, advice, assist and befriend. Some elements of the community saw that as being 'soft' on crime but it always meant that the offender had to face up to what they had done.

Prison was the escape from responsibility and it still is, as well as costing so much more in both money and human life. A person once imprisoned is a greater risk to the community than one who is kept in the community. Yes, prison is needed for those who remain a threat to the community but being a nuisance to others is never a good reason for a custodial sentence. Tariffing has, in my opinion, caused far more damage than it could ever solve.

Probation was about crime prevention. Rarely did my 'success rate', that is orders that completed without further offending, fall below eighty per cent. We provided a first-class service to the courts by our reports and we kept people out of prison and contributing to their community.

Sadly, we were also a political pawn and one Home Secretary who did not like us, wiped out our social work training at the stroke of his pen. Prevention, as I have already said is the prime reason for probation and facing your responsibilities is more challenging to the offender than anything the court might do. The present attitude seems designed to fill the prisons rather than pursue justice for either victim or offender.

As such I am glad to see how reparation schemes have developed. Where appropriate, they are of great value to both victim and offender.

The prison population is now more than double when I retired even though the numbers going through court are much the same. The probation service has effectively been emasculated and sentencing become tariff based instead of a system of common sense and justice. This has been caused by both recent governments

That makes the stories of some of the people that I have met on my way as, if not more relevant for today as they were in the 1970s/80s. It is from this era of my work that the stories come as it is most unlikely that anyone would now be recognised.

Anyway, I have changed the names and basic details. Only the story is unchanged. It was a great privilege to be there at a time when justice was the target and not the cost. In these few pages, you will have met some of the people called criminals. After over thirty years working with them, I still wonder who the victim is. The poor, the inadequate, the ill-educated, are there in abundance. But so are the victims of crime and the prime work of probation was always the prevention of crime for both victim and perpetrator.

I was fortunate to be there when the answers were about trying to change things for the better and I say again what a privilege it was to be where I could be part of the humane side of criminal justice.